THE MEANING OF GIFTS

Stories from Turkey

Life is full of things to make you smile, and things to make you cry. And they are all here in these stories. In the first story we see how difficult it is, in a small house, to have guests who stay a long time – a very long time . . . Then we meet Guldiken, who is telling his mother about his day at school, but how can she understand? City life is very different from life in a village . . . In the next story, Unal must stay in bed because he has measles, but across the road is a wonderful toy shop . . . And when the little hunters at the lake shoot their first bird, they are very excited – until they learn what kind of bird it is . . .

BOOKWORMS WORLD STORIES

English has become an international language, and is used on every continent, in many varieties, for all kinds of purposes. *Bookworms World Stories* are the latest addition to the Oxford Bookworms Library. Their aim is to bring the best of the world's stories to the English language learner, and to celebrate the use of English for storytelling all around the world.

Jennifer Bassett
Series Editor

OXFORD BOOKWORMS LIBRARY

World Stories

The Meaning of Gifts

Stories from Turkey

Stage 1 (400 headwords)

Series Editor: Jennifer Bassett
Founder Editor: Tricia Hedge
Activities Editors: Jennifer Bassett and Christine Lindop

RETOLD BY JENNIFER BASSETT

The Meaning of Gifts

Stories from Turkey

Illustrated by
Gay Galsworthy

OXFORD UNIVERSITY PRESS

OXFORD
UNIVERSITY PRESS

Great Clarendon Street, Oxford OX2 6DP

Oxford University Press is a department of the University of Oxford.
It furthers the University's objective of excellence in research, scholarship,
and education by publishing worldwide in

Oxford New York

Auckland Cape Town Dar es Salaam Hong Kong Karachi
Kuala Lumpur Madrid Melbourne Mexico City Nairobi
New Delhi Shanghai Taipei Toronto

With offices in

Argentina Austria Brazil Chile Czech Republic France Greece
Guatemala Hungary Italy Japan Poland Portugal Singapore
South Korea Switzerland Thailand Turkey Ukraine Vietnam

OXFORD and OXFORD ENGLISH are registered trade marks of
Oxford University Press in the UK and in certain other countries

ISBN 978 0 19 478927 1

A complete recording of this Bookworms edition of
The Meaning of Gifts: Stories from Turkey is available on
audio CD ISBN 978 0 19 478862 5

Printed in China

ACKNOWLEDGEMENTS
Translations from Turkish by:
Sylvia Seden (*The Guests, The Horse of Death*)
Sema Özkaya (*The Picture of the Year 2000, The Little Hunters at the Lake*)
Illustrated by: Gay Galsworthy

Word count (main text): 5,254 words

For more information on the Oxford Bookworms Library,
visit www.oup.com/bookworms

CONTENTS

The Guests

HUSEYIN RAHMI GURPINAR

Retold by Jennifer Bassett

When guests come to stay in your house, it makes a lot of work. There are meals to cook, food to buy, washing to do, beds to make . . . It all takes time and money.

Izzet Efendi and his family are very happy to have guests to stay. When your friends need help, you must help them, but these friends stay and stay . . . and stay.

Nineteen days and nineteen nights. That was a long time, a very long time, in a small house. There were four people – husband, wife, and two children . . . four guests. And they ate. Every day they ate bread, so that was two okkas more bread every day. Bread, meat, vegetables – they all cost money.

And of course they needed a room. There were not many rooms in the house. That was difficult for the host family too.

But the guests did not understand. Perhaps they did not want to understand. They saw the angry faces of the host family, and they smiled – just smiled and smiled.

The husband of the guest family, Halil Efendi, drank

Every day they ate bread . . . Bread, meat, vegetables
– they all cost money.

raki every night too. His host, Izzet Efendi, was a religious
man and he never drank alcohol. He didn't even like the
smell of it, but every evening Halil Efendi came home
with a small bottle of raki and some olives in a piece of
paper. Then he sat and drank and ate and talked, very
happily, until evening prayers.

So dinner was always late, because of course Izzet
Efendi could not begin to eat without Halil Efendi. Izzet
Efendi did not like waiting for his dinner, and every
evening he got hungrier – and angrier.

After five or six days of this, he spoke very openly to
his guest.

'Efendi, every evening you come home with a bottle of
raki in your pocket. Is that right?'

But his guest understood the question in a very different
way.

'My friend,' he said. 'You are very kind to me and my family. You welcome us into your house, and it is not easy for you. I know that, and I am very grateful to you. But now, what are you saying? Do you want to buy my raki for me? No, no, I cannot take more from you. I must buy my raki, not you. Please.'

Izzet Efendi looked at his guest's smiling face. 'But . . .

Every evening Halil Efendi sat and drank and ate and talked, very happily.

but I didn't mean . . .' he began. Then he stopped. What could he say?

Halil Efendi was just a clerk in a government office in Anadolu Kavagi, but he and his family had very little money. So they came to Istanbul to visit the money-lenders. Money-lenders are expensive. They give you money, but later they want more money back – much more. Every day Halil Efendi went to all the money-lenders and tried to find some cheaper money, but he couldn't. And so he and his family stayed in Izzet Efendi's home – and stayed and stayed.

👓 👓 👓

One day the host family had a meeting. They all went into a room, closed the door carefully, and began to talk.

'I'm afraid to look in the storeroom,' said the oldest lady of the house. 'All our food for the winter – where is it now? Inside those hungry guests! They never stop eating! And they never say thank you! And those children – my God, they eat more than their parents!'

'Ah, my dear lady,' said Zarafet. 'Don't look in the storeroom. There's no more olive oil, no rice or sugar, no beans. There's nothing! The dogs and cats in the street stop eating when they are full, but those children never stop. They come to me in the kitchen and say, "Nanny, is the food ready yet? Can we eat now? We're so hungry." Sometimes I get angry and shout, "Get out of here! I don't like children in the kitchen. Out!" One day I chased them

Sometimes I get angry and shout, 'Get out of here!
I don't like children in the kitchen. Out!'

with a piece of burning wood from the fire, and their mother was angry with me. Ah! I cannot live with these people! I spend hours cooking my imambayildi, and those children come and put their dirty fingers into it, then put their fingers in their mouths, then back in the food again. And that man – drinking raki all the evening! Then he stands in front of the open window and sings. The man in the next house is very ill, and our guest stands there, singing! And the house, the kitchen, everything, smells of raki all the time. Ugh!'

Suddenly Cezalet Hanim, the daughter of the house, looked at the door. 'Sshh, Nanny, talk quietly,' she said. 'There's a noise out there. Perhaps that woman is listening to us.'

But Zarafet did not want to talk quietly, and she began to shout. 'She can listen. Why not? I'm not afraid. I tell her these things every day, but she doesn't want to hear. It's a nice life for our guests – food, beds, drinking, singing . . . Wonderful!'

'Be quiet, Nanny,' said Cezalet Hanim. 'I want to talk now.'

'Talk, my child, talk,' said Zarafet. 'You can talk for forty days and forty nights, but what can you do about our terrible guests?'

'Listen to this,' Cezalet Hanim said. 'On their second day here the lady said to me, "Oh, I am going out. Please, can I wear your chador and your shoes? My shoes hurt my feet, you see." Now why does she want to wear my chador? Why can't she wear *her* chador?'

'That's easy,' said Zarafet. 'At one time people gave the family money to help them, and she doesn't want those people to see her. So she wears *your* chador, and nobody knows her when she goes out. Oh yes, she's very clever.'

'She does it all the time,' said Cezalet Hanim. 'When

Zarafet began to shout, 'It's a nice life for our guests – food, beds, drinking, singing . . . Wonderful!'

she goes out, she always wears my chador and my shoes. I cry when I see my shoes now – they look so old and tired.'

'She takes your shoes and your chador,' said Zarafet. 'But what does she ask me for? Pants! She comes all the way from Kavaklar with only one pair of underpants? Does she think I have hundreds of pairs of pants? She took a pair of my nice pants, and she wore them and wore them. And when she gave them back – ugh! They were so dirty. I just can't talk about it.'

The oldest lady of the house put her head in her hands. 'What are we going to do?' she asked. 'Are they ever going to leave?'

'They came here because they wanted to get money from the money-lenders,' said Zarafet. 'Where is that money now?'

Suddenly, there was a knock on the door.

'Who is it?' said the oldest lady of the house.

'It's her, of course,' said Zarafet. 'Our guest.'

'Please open the door,' said the person outside the room.

Zarafet opened the door. There, with two big bags and her two children, stood their guest, dressed in her chador. Her face was very unhappy and her eyes were red from crying.

'I am here to say goodbye, ladies,' she said. 'I'm so sorry. You are very, very kind to us, and we give you so much trouble. Thank you for having us in your house. We are so grateful. Please, don't be angry with us.'

Her hosts looked at their guest's unhappy face and her red eyes. What could they say?

'You are always welcome. Our home is your home.
For a few weeks – or for forty years.'

'Ah, my dear,' said the oldest lady of the house. 'You don't give us any trouble. Of course not. You are *always* welcome. Our home is *your* home. For a few weeks – or for forty years. What does it matter? Please don't be unhappy.'

'Is something wrong?' said Cezalet Hanim. 'How can you leave us so suddenly? No, no, you must stay. Of course you must stay. Now, take off your chador and sit down. Don't go!'

And then Zarafet spoke. 'What do you mean? You can't go now, my dear! No, no, no!' She began to cry a little. 'Aaah! You are our family, too. You can't go away and leave us. No, no.' She put her hands on the children's heads. 'Ah, my dear children. Come to the kitchen with me. Your nanny is going to cook you a wonderful dinner today . . .'

The Picture of the Year 2000

AYSE KILIMCI

Retold by Jennifer Bassett

City life and village life are very different, and sometimes it is hard to change from one to the other. Perhaps it is easier to make the change when you are young.

Guldiken and his mother are now living in the city, and Guldiken comes home from school to tell his mother all about his day. But his mother cannot forget her mountain village, and she finds it hard to understand the strange ways of city people . . .

'So today was the day to take gifts to your teacher,' said the woman.

Her voice was not happy, was not unhappy, was not angry, was not pleased. It showed nothing. But she *felt* angry. She felt angry in her heart. But with what? She did not know.

'Everybody brought something for the teacher,' said the boy. 'Everybody.'

'But you don't know anything about the city yet,' said the woman in her colourless voice. 'Did you tell your teacher that?'

*'Your city sky is new to us, your rain is strange,
we don't know your birds.'*

'No, I didn't,' said the boy.

'We came here to the city only a short time ago. Did you tell her that? We are still looking back to our village. Your city sky is new to us, your rain is strange, we don't know your birds. Did you tell her all these things?'

'No.'

'Did you tell her this? "My mother was afraid when she brought me to the school, because her shoes were old and her clothes were different. She was afraid of the school, of the people, of the crowd, of all that noise, of all those women – they know so much. My mother could not speak because her voice was afraid to come out. Her heart is silent and afraid. In our village my mother was queen of the mountains, she was strong, she understood everything. Here, in your place, she is nothing, she understands nothing, she is queen of nothing." Did you tell her all this?'

'How can these city people know about your village, mother?' said the boy.

'Did you tell her this? "Look, teacher, my mother can shoot well, my mother can cut wood for the winter fires in two minutes. My father can work all day in the fields and he does not get tired." Did you tell her these things?'

'No, I didn't.'

'So today was the day to take gifts to teachers. You can play a flute beautifully. It is more beautiful than a bird

'In our village my mother was queen of the mountains,
she was strong, she understood everything.'

*'My mother can cut wood for the winter fires in two minutes.
My father can work all day in the fields.'*

singing, and all the sheep in the village stop and listen to you. Didn't you tell her that? You can ride a horse, you can find water under the winter snow. Why didn't you tell her these things?'

'What does a city teacher understand about these things?'

'But you must tell her. In the city, you must tell people that we can do these things.'

'Mum, it's OK. I had some money and I bought a gift for the teacher.'

'Where did you find the money?'

'It was my pocket money. I didn't spend it all, so I had a little money for a gift.'

'You can play a flute beautifully. All the sheep
in the village stop and listen to you.'

'What did you buy? For a city teacher, it must be something good.'

'It is. It is something white, white as milk, quiet as the sky above our mountains.'

'Come on, tell me. What is it?'

'No. You tell me. Think about it.'

'Look, here is my hand, and it is coming down on your head now.'

'I bought her a nice piece of parchment.'

'A what?'

'A pie–e–e–ce of parchment!'

'What is that?'

'Paper, Mum, paper. You write on it, with a pen or a pencil. You write letters and send them far away to different places. It's different from the pages in a notebook.'

'Oh, what a wonderful son you are! You are nearly a man, I can see. You save money, and you can go and buy a gift for your teacher. Oh, I'm so happy! What did the teacher say when she got the paper. Was she happy?'

'She said, "Guldiken, what do you want?"'

'What does that mean?'

'She didn't understand, Mum. She looked at me strangely. And then she said, "Sit down, Guldiken. Don't walk around."'

'So . . .?'

'My piece of parchment was my gift, but she didn't

*'Gifts must be flowers, or something heavy and beautiful.
City teachers don't understand other gifts.'*

understand that. Gifts must be flowers, or something
heavy and beautiful. City teachers don't understand
other gifts.'

'So you bought her a gift and she didn't understand
it. Oh, these city people! They have big houses and long
streets and gardens, but they don't understand a child's
gift.'

'It's OK, Mum.'

'It's not OK. With your money, you bought a white
piece of parchment for her and she cannot understand
this. What gifts can she understand? We can find many
good gifts without money – a cup of fresh milk or a
flower from the mountain – but city people can never

*'So, tell me about the time when we are all dead and you are
a big important man in your world.'*

understand gifts like that. But you are wrong. You did not
tell her about the important things. You always find the
best fruit on the tree, you always know the fastest horse.
You are clever at these things.'

'It's OK, Mum. The teacher said, "Guldiken, it's a nice
piece of parchment and you can draw a picture on it." We
drew pictures today, Mum.'

'What pictures?'

'There's a picture competition for all the schools. The teacher wanted us all to draw a picture of the year 2000.'

'What is that?'

'It's a long time from today. The picture of the time when you are dead and Dad is dead and I am a father and have children.'

'So, tell me about the time when we are all dead and you are a big important man in your world.'

'The teacher wanted us to imagine the world and the mountains and the cities and our homes and everything.'

'How can you know about those things? You can't see them now.'

'She said "imagine", Mum.'

'And . . .?'

'Everybody in the class talked about different things – computers, videos, cars. I don't know those things.'

'Didn't you ask them?'

'It's difficult to tell you, Mum. I know them, but it's so difficult. I cannot imagine the year 2000. I can only think of today. So I drew something beautiful on my white piece of parchment.'

'What?'

'I drew a sun – a very big, red, hot sun, in the middle of the paper. My sun was bright, bright red. You couldn't look at it, Mum. It was so hot and red and bright.'

'Good for you, Guldiken.'

'And the teacher asked, "What is it?" And I told her, "You wanted us to draw the year 2000, teacher. So I drew the sun in the year 2000." It was huge, Mum – a huge, red, hot, bright sun. That is the best thing to draw for the year 2000.'

'The sun is the best thing to draw for the year 2000.'

The Horse of Death

SAIT FAIK

Retold by Jennifer Bassett

*Little Unal has measles and must stay in bed.
But the sun is shining, and from his window
he can see the toy shop across the road. There
are so many toys in that shop – big, small, in
all colours! But the most wonderful toy is a
horse, a big black horse with a long tail and
lights in its eyes.*

*More than anything in the world, Unal wants
to ride that horse . . .*

Little Unal was ill. He had the measles and so he was in bed. But he was bored. 'What can I do?' he thought. 'The doctor says I can't go out, but the sun is shining and it's a beautiful day!'

That morning, when his mother left the house, she said to Unal's grandmother, 'The sun is shining but it's very cold. Be careful with Unal, Mother. We don't want him to catch cold.'

From his window Unal could look out at the street. And when his grandmother came into his room, Unal was at the window, wearing only his pyjamas.

'What did your mother tell you?' said his grandmother.

When his grandmother came into his room, Unal was
at the window, wearing only his pyjamas.

'And what did the doctor say? Do you want to catch cold,
and die, like your grandfather? Come now, go back to
bed.'

'Grandma, what beautiful weather! And I'm not ill. I
haven't got a fever.'

'No, thank God, you haven't got a fever. But it's easy
to catch cold. And then those red spots on your face are
going to go inside you.'

'Good!' said Unal.

'No, it's not good. Those red spots can kill you, so you
must be careful. Come now, get back into bed.'

Unal got back into bed, and his grandmother went back to the kitchen.

Unal's father was dead. He died before Unal was born. Now his grandfather was dead too, so Unal had nobody to call 'father'. His mother worked as a cleaning woman in the government offices in the town. It was not a good job and the family did not have much money.

During that day, Unal was sometimes in bed, and sometimes at the window. When his grandmother came into the room, Unal got back into bed. When she left, he ran back to the window.

Across the street there was a toy shop, and Unal watched it from his window. Today was New Year's Day and there were bright lights in the toy shop window. What wonderful toys there were – animals and cars, big and small, in all colours! But the most wonderful thing was a black horse. Oh, Unal wanted that horse so much! When you pulled the reins, there were lights in the horse's eyes. Three of its feet were white, and it had a long brown mane.

Unal stood at the window, thinking, imagining. 'Now I'm riding that black horse,' he said to himself. 'I'm not ill. There's nothing wrong with me – of course there isn't. When I'm riding the black horse, I don't get cold, I'm not ill, and there are no red spots on my face.'

Then he heard his grandmother at the door, and he ran back to bed.

But the most wonderful thing was a black horse.
Oh, Unal wanted that horse so much!

When his grandmother came in, she said, 'That's a good boy, Unal! Stay in bed, and you can have something nice for dinner tonight. Now, I've still got a lot of work to do in the kitchen. Remember – don't get out of bed.' She went out and closed the door.

It was now dark and all the lights of the toy shop window shone brightly across the street. Unal got up and dressed, then left his room quietly. He couldn't find his shoes, but he found some old shoes of his grandmother's and put those on. He ran out into the street, and across to the toy shop.

There were a lot of women in the shop, with their children. Everybody bought toys for their children on New Year's Day. Unal didn't have any toys, but he didn't want them. He wanted that black horse. He wanted to ride it just one time. The shopkeeper was busy, everybody was busy. Nobody looked at a small eight-year-old boy.

Unal went in and walked quietly around the shop, looking at things. Then he hid behind some big boxes, and waited.

Some time later, all the lights went out and the shopkeeper closed the doors and went away. The street lights outside shone into the shop. Unal went to the shop window and slowly opened the big glass door. Then he got into the window and climbed on to the back of the black horse. He pulled the reins, then looked at the horse's head. Yes, there were lights, bright shining lights, in the horse's eyes.

Unal began to ride. 'I can see snow on the ground all around me,' he said to himself. 'I can see clouds in the

*'I can see clouds in the sky above, and silvery lights
from the moon. Everything is so bright, so cold.'*

sky above, and silvery lights from the moon. Everything is so bright, so cold. I feel I am swimming in the sea, but the water is as cold as ice.'

He and the horse rode on. Then Unal began to feel warm again. Far away there was a light – the colour of Unal's blond hair. The horse rode on towards the yellow light.

It was the sun. Now Unal began to burn – his hair, his hands, everything was on fire. The black horse, too, burned like fire.

Then everything changed again. Unal felt strange, empty – first he was in deep water, then he was in the sky. He was not hot, or cold; he did not feel anything. He and his horse began to go faster – faster and faster . . .

When Unal's grandmother next went to his room, Unal wasn't there. His grandmother was very afraid. She looked for him in the house, in the street, and she asked everybody:

'Where is Unal?'

But nobody knew. Other families in the street came to help, and people ran in and out of the house all night. Then, when morning arrived, a man came to the women in front of Unal's house.

'Look,' he said. 'Look there – in the window of the toy shop.'

Everybody ran to look. They saw a small boy on the

They saw a small boy on the back of the black horse.
But he was dead, cold and dead.

back of the black horse, with a smile on his face. But he was dead, cold and dead.

They broke the shop window and tried to take Unal off the horse, but they could not move him. Unal belonged to the black horse now. He could not stop riding, riding, riding . . .

They took him home, still on the horse. His grandmother looked and looked at the child's blue face.

'Ah, Unal!' she said. 'What did the doctor tell you? Those red spots can kill people when they catch cold.'

Then a woman from the next house spoke. 'When somebody wants to ride the black horse of death, nobody can stop him.'

They buried Unal and the black horse together in the cold ground.

The Little Hunters at the Lake

YALVAC URAL

Retold by Jennifer Bassett

Young boys often want to do the same things as their fathers. So Hikmet secretly borrows his father's big hunting gun, and he and his three friends go down to the lake. They are excited, laughing, making big plans to shoot ducks and cook them over a fire. They think they are hunters now, just like the men. But they are only boys, and still have a lot to learn . . .

The sky above the little lake was full of birds – small birds, big birds, birds of all colours. We sat in the rain by Hikmet's garden wall and watched them.

'Winter's coming,' I said to my friends. 'The birds are beginning to leave and fly away to warm countries.'

Then a hunting dog came by. It stopped and smelled all of us, then went away.

'Is that Tekin's dog from the village?' asked Peker.

'Yes, it is,' said Hikmet. 'But what's it doing here in the rain?'

'Perhaps the hunters are coming out to the lake,' I said.

*'The birds are beginning to leave and fly away
to warm countries.'*

Then we saw them. There was Tekin, the driver Nuri,
Halil, and two more men. They wore hunting clothes and
carried guns. We all wanted to go with them. Peker spoke
for all of us.

'I'd like to have a gun and be a hunter, too,' he said.

Then Hikmet got up and ran into his house. He came
back with something in a bag under his arm.

'What is it?' we said, but we already knew.

Hikmet opened the bag and we looked at the long, beautiful gun.

'Hey, that's wonderful!'

'Of course it is!'

'How much is it?'

'Forty thousand.'

'Wow!'

'*We've got five bullets,*' *Hikmet said.* '*So we can all*
shoot once. Then I can shoot a second time . . .'

'Your father's going to be angry.'

'Yes. But I can put the gun back before he comes home.'

'OK,' we all said, and began to walk to the lake. First Hikmet carried the gun, then me, then Peker, and then Muammer. We were all hunters now.

'We've got five bullets,' Hikmet said. 'So we can all shoot once. Then I can shoot a second time, with the fifth bullet, because I brought the gun.'

'And when we've got five dead birds, we can cook them and eat them,' said Peker.

At the lake we could see the hunters and hear the noise of their dogs. We, too, waited by the lake and watched. It rained, and stopped, then rained again. But there were no birds on the lake or in the sky – not one.

We waited, but then we began to think about Hikmet's angry father.

'Shall we go home now and put the gun back?' said Muammer.

Suddenly, we saw three ducks. They flew down to the ground not far from us. Hikmet stood up quietly and tried to shoot one of them. He didn't hit it, of course, and the ducks flew away. But the gun made a very loud noise, and now the sky was full of thousands of birds!

During the day the birds hide around the lake, and the hunters wait for the evening before they begin to shoot. But we learned all this later.

Three ducks flew down to the ground not far from us.

Now the birds were afraid because of the noise. They all flew away and so the hunters had nothing to shoot.

The hunters began to chase us, shouting angrily. But we could run faster, and so we escaped. Soon we stopped, and began to talk and laugh.

'Where's our duck dinner, then?' said Muammer.

I laughed. 'Wait until tomorrow,' I said. 'Or the next day – when Hikmet can shoot!'

'Hunters don't always come home with lots of dead birds,' said Hikmet. 'Listen. The birdseller Ali shoots birds. And who does he sell them to?'

'To the hunters!' Peker said.

'Right!' Hikmet said. 'And why? Because people laugh at hunters when they come home with nothing. So the hunters go quietly to Ali, buy his dead birds, and then they can talk about all their exciting hunts!'

Suddenly I saw some birds in the sky. 'Be quiet,' I told

my friends. I took the gun, put a bullet in it, and waited. When the birds were right above me, I shot. Two birds fell out of the sky and down to the ground. Shouting happily, we ran to the place. But just then, one of the birds flew back up from the ground, high into the sky. We were very surprised.

We soon found the other bird. It was big, with a long neck. Hikmet looked at it.

We soon found the other bird. It was big,
with a long neck.

'It's dead,' he said.

'The second bird was only hurt, perhaps,' said Muammer.

We looked carefully at the dead bird, but we all felt a little afraid. Was it really dead? High in the sky above us, the second bird flew round and round in circles, giving long, sad cries.

We began to carry our dead bird home, and after a time the bird in the sky flew away.

'When are we going to eat this bird?' asked Muammer.

'Tomorrow,' said Hikmet.

'Who's going to cook it?'

'We are!'

'But we don't know how!'

'Let's go to the birdseller Ali and ask him.'

We put the gun back in Hikmet's house and ran to Ali's shop. There were a lot of dead birds in the shop, but our bird was different.

'Hello, boys,' Ali said. 'What can I do for you?'

'We shot a bird,' we said, 'but what is it, and how do we cook it?'

Ali smiled. 'Well, you boys are better hunters than the men!'

We put the bag with our bird on Ali's table and opened it. Ali stopped smiling. He quickly put the bird back into the bag, and for a minute or two he said nothing. Then he said, 'Look, children, you don't understand.

You can't eat this bird! Take it back, and bury it in the ground.'

We looked at him with our mouths open in surprise.

Then Ali asked, 'Was his mate with him there?'

'There was another bird, but it flew away,' said Hikmet.

'Good,' said Ali, and smiled. He began to say something, but stopped.

'Did we really do something terrible?' asked Hikmet.

'Listen,' said Ali. 'These birds are called cranes – you know, the famous "crane" in our songs. Hunters never shoot them because they are the "symbols of love".'

We did not understand this, but we understood the words 'take it back and bury it'. It was nearly dark, but we went back to the lake and found the right place. Then

*'You can't eat this bird!' said Ali. 'Take it back,
and bury it in the ground.'*

we dug a hole and buried our crane there. I think we all cried a little, because we felt so sad.

⚘

After that day we never talked about hunting. We had a long cold winter that year. In the spring, we began to play outside again, but there was still some snow on the ground.

'Let's go and look at our crane's grave,' Hikmet said one day.

We all wanted to do this, but Hikmet was the first to say the words. We walked quietly to the lake, then Peker said, 'I asked Dad about "symbols of love" one day.'

'And what does it mean?' asked Muammer.

'It means that cranes know how to love. Their love is the best and the strongest in the world.'

There was still snow on our crane's grave, but we could see two snowdrops too. Snowdrops are always the first flowers of spring. Hikmet began to move the snow away from the top of the grave, but suddenly he stopped. There was something under the snow. Then we saw it.

It was our crane. It lay there on the ground, icy cold, on top of its grave. We felt very sad.

'Who took it out?' said Peker.

'Perhaps it was wild dogs,' answered Hikmet. 'And then they couldn't eat it because it was frozen.'

'Oh, why didn't we dig a deeper hole?' Muammer cried.

'We can do that now,' said Hikmet. 'God stopped the wild dogs from eating our crane, so now we must bury it deeper.'

Sadly, we began to dig. Soon the hole was open, but then we suddenly saw something, and stopped very quickly. There was *another* crane in the hole. We looked at it, and felt afraid. Nobody could speak.

Hikmet took our crane out. Then he put it on the ground and began to cry. We all cried too, but we did not know why.

Hikmet stood up. 'I was afraid of this,' he said, 'and I didn't want it to happen.'

There was another *crane in the hole. We looked at it, and felt afraid.*

We did not understand.

'Cranes, symbols of love, please forgive us,' Hikmet said quietly. Then he looked at us. 'Cranes are very loving birds,' he said, 'and the male and the female stay together all their lives. Cranes always live in warm places, but when a crane dies, its mate goes to a cold snowy place. Then it dies in the snow, and nobody can eat it. People do not eat birds that die in this way. And hunters never shoot cranes because they know all these things.'

Our hearts were very sad. We buried the two birds together in the hole and put snowdrops all over their grave. And after that day, every time we heard the word 'love', we thought about the cranes.

And we never forgot to go to the grave every spring.

One spring morning when I woke up, I saw a pair of cranes at my window. I ran to the window, but they flew away. Then I saw some snowdrops there. I took the flowers in my hand, held them to my face, and began to cry. Some minutes later, I heard someone at the door.

Hikmet was there, his eyes red from crying. There were snowdrops in his hand too.

'They forgive us,' Hikmet said. 'The cranes forgive us.'

GLOSSARY

belong if something is yours, it belongs to you

blond a very light yellow colour (e.g. blond hair)

bright giving out a lot of light

bury to put a dead person in the ground

busy working, with a lot of things to do

buy (past tense **bought**) to get something for money

catch cold to get ill with a cold

chador a long garment worn over the head and body by Muslim women when they go outside

clerk someone who works in an office, writing letters, etc.

clever quick to understand and learn; not stupid

colourless without colour or (in this story) showing no feeling

competition a game, sport, test, etc. which people try to win

death dying; the end of life

dig (past tense **dug**) to make a hole in the ground

draw (past tense **drew**) to make pictures with a pen, pencil, etc.

Efendi a polite Turkish word to use when you speak to a man

fall (past tense **fell**) to go quickly from a high place to a low place

female a woman, or animal, bird, etc. that can have babies

fever an illness when you feel very hot

fly (past tense **flew**) to move through the air, not on the ground

forgive to show that you are not angry with someone any more

frozen (*adj*) very, very cold and hard like ice

gift something that you give to someone (e.g. on their birthday)

government the people that control a country or a city

grateful thankful; showing thanks

grave a hole in the ground for a dead person

ground what you stand or walk on

guest somebody who stays in another person's house

heart   your heart pushes the blood round your body

heavy   not easy to lift or move

hide (past tense **hid**)   to be in a place where people cannot see you

host   somebody who has guests in their house

huge   very, very big

hunt   to chase and kill animals and birds

hurt   to give pain to someone or something

ice   water that is hard (frozen) because it is very cold

imagine   to have a picture of something in your head

imambayildi   a cooked vegetable dish of aubergine, onions, and tomatoes

kind (*adj*)   friendly; good to other people

lady   a woman

male   a male animal, bird, or person cannot have babies

mate   an animal or bird that is the 'husband' or 'wife' of another

measles   an illness with small red spots on the skin

pair   something with two parts (e.g. a pair of trousers)

parchment   a special kind of 'paper' made from animal skins

pocket money   money that parents give to a child each week

prayer   speaking to God

queen   a woman from a royal family who rules a country

raki   a strong alcoholic drink in Turkey

religious   believing in God and doing the right things for your religion

sad   not happy

shine (past tense **shone**)   to send out light; to be bright

silent   with no sound; not speaking

smell   you smell with your nose

spots   small places on the skin which are red and sore

storeroom   a room where you keep things (e.g. food) to use later

strange   unusual or surprising; that you do not know

strong able to move heavy things or do hard work easily

surprised you are surprised when something strange or unusual happens

symbol something which is a sign or mark for another thing (e.g. the sign ? is the written symbol for a question)

terrible very bad

trouble problems, difficulties

voice the sound that you make when you speak

ACTIVITIES

Before Reading

Before you read the stories, read the introductions at the beginning. Then use the activities here to help you think about the stories. What's going to happen in them? How much can you guess?

1 *The Guests* (story introduction page 1). Choose an answer for each question.

   1 In the end, how long do the guests stay?
     a) three weeks   c) a year
     b) two months   d) we don't know
   2 Are the two families still speaking at the end of the story?
     YES / NO

2 *The Picture of the Year 2000* (story introduction page 11). Choose an answer for each question.

   1 At school Guldiken gives his teacher a gift. What is it?
     a) some flowers   c) a book
     b) a piece of paper   d) some chocolate
   2 When Guldiken tells his mother about his day at school, what does she do or how does she feel?
     a) She laughs a lot.   c) She is pleased with him.
     b) She is surprised.   d) She is angry with him.

3 *The Horse of Death* (story introduction page 21). **Choose one of these ideas.**

1 Unal's mother buys the black horse and gives it to Unal.

2 Unal's grandmother gives Unal a different toy.

3 Unal rides the black horse secretly one night.

4 Another family buys the black horse for their child.

4 *The Little Hunters at the Lake* (story introduction page 30). **Choose an answer for each question.**

1 What do the little hunters do with their first bird?

   a) They bury it.   c) They eat it.

   b) They hide it.   d) They sell it.

2 The boys learn a lesson that day. What is it about?

   a) About guns.   c) About love.

   b) About shooting.   d) About cooking.

5 **These twelve words are all from the stories. Which stories do they belong to? Put them into the table below (three words for each story). Use the glossary and a dictionary to help you.**

bullet / fever / fields / flowers / grateful / gun /
host / ill / mountains / shoot / spots / welcome

The Guests	
The Picture of the Year 2000	
The Horse of Death	
The Little Hunters at the Lake	

ACTIVITIES

After Reading

1 **Match these halves of sentences to make a summary of *The Guests*. Use these linking words to join your sentences.**

and / and / because / but / so / so / when

1 Halil Efendi wanted to visit the money-lenders,

2 Izzet Efendi only had a small house,

3 After nineteen days, the host family felt angry

4 One day, the women of the host family began to talk about their guests,

5 _____ Zarafet opened the door,

6 She thanked the ladies of the house,

7 The host family couldn't say, 'Go away! Goodbye!',

8 _____ the wife of Halil Efendi heard their angry voices.

9 Halil Efendi's wife was there with her children, ready to leave.

10 _____ he brought his family to Istanbul.

11 _____ said they were very, very kind.

12 _____ they said, 'You must stay, dear friends!'

13 _____ he welcomed Halil Efendi's family into it.

14 _____ their guests ate lots of food and never said thank you.

2 In *The Picture of the Year 2000*, perhaps Guldiken's teacher wrote in her diary after school that day. Use these words to fill in the gaps.

ago, beautiful, came, children, different, flowers, for, huge, in, me, mountains, or, pictures, piece, teachers, What, Why

Today all the _____ brought gifts for their _____. There were lots of _____ and other _____ things. One little boy, Guldiken, gave _____ something strange – a _____ of parchment. I didn't understand. _____ did he do that? Of course, Guldiken _____ to the city only a few weeks _____. Before that, he lived _____ a village in the _____. Life is very _____ there, I think.

All the children drew _____ of the year 2000 today _____ a competition. Guldiken didn't draw a computer _____ a car – he drew a _____ red sun. _____ a strange boy!

3 Did you like the ending in *The Horse of Death*? Choose words in this passage to make two different endings for the story, one beginning with the shopkeeper, and one with Unal's grandmother. Which ending do you like best? Explain why.

1 The shopkeeper . . .
2 Unal's grandmother . . .

   . . . found Unal on the black horse. *He / She* felt *sorry for / angry with* Unal, and *shouted at him / gave him the black horse.* Unal felt very *happy / sad* after that. A week later, he *got better / died*, and *the shopkeeper / his grandmother cried / smiled a lot.*

4 Here is Peker (from *The Little Hunters at the Lake*) talking to his father. Put their conversation in the right order and write in the speakers' names. Peker speaks first (number 3).

1 _____ 'Ali the birdseller. But what does it mean, Dad?'

2 _____ 'Its mate is very unhappy. So don't ever shoot a crane, Peker.'

3 _____ 'Dad, do hunters ever shoot cranes?'

4 _____ 'Symbols of love? Who told you that?'

5 _____ 'No, Peker. People never kill cranes.'

6 _____ 'No, Dad, of course not!'

7 _____ 'It means that cranes are very loving birds. They know how to love. A crane never leaves its mate, you see. They stay together until death.'

8 _____ 'Why don't they? Is it because cranes are symbols of love?'

9 _____ 'Do they? But what happens when somebody shoots – I mean, when one of the cranes dies?'

5 Complete this passage about cranes with these words.

big, cold, female, grey, lives, long, male, necks, warm

Cranes are _____ birds. They are usually _____, and have long _____ and _____ legs. When the _____ weather comes, they fly away to _____ countries. The _____ and the _____ stay together all their _____.

6 Find these words in the word search below, and draw a line through them. Words go from left to right, and from top to bottom.

bullet, city, cloud, flute, frozen, gift, grave, guest, gun, hole, horse, hunt, mate, measles, moon, mountains, neck, sheep, symbol, trouble, village, wall, wood

G	I	F	T	T	C	H	W	O	O	D	F
E	H	L	V	I	L	L	A	G	E	C	R
M	O	U	G	H	O	C	L	R	A	I	O
E	L	T	R	O	U	B	L	E	N	T	Z
A	E	E	A	R	D	U	E	G	H	Y	E
S	S	F	V	S	O	L	N	U	U	R	N
L	S	H	E	E	P	L	E	E	N	M	G
E	I	V	M	A	T	E	C	S	T	O	E
S	Y	M	B	O	L	T	K	T	U	O	S
G	U	N	M	O	U	N	T	A	I	N	S

Now write down all the letters that don't have a line through them. Begin with the first line and go across each line to the end. There are 18 letters, which make a sentence of 4 words.

1 What is the sentence?
2 Which story does it come from?
3 Who said it?
4 What did he have in his hand when he said it?
5 Do you think he was happy or unhappy, or both? Why do you think that?

7 **What did you think about these stories? Choose some names and make some sentences about them.**

the (host/guest) family / Guldiken / Guldiken's (mother/ teacher) / Unal / Unal's grandmother / the little hunters / the cranes

1 I liked (didn't like) _____ because _____.

2 I felt sorry (pleased) for _____ when _____.

3 _____ was (were) right (wrong) to _____.

8 **Here is a short poem (a kind of poem called a haiku) about one of the stories. Which of the four stories is it about?**

> New to the city,
> a boy chooses the wrong gift,
> but how could he know?

> Leaving a village
> for life in a city is
> a hard change to make.

Here is another haiku, about the same story.

A haiku is a Japanese poem, which is always in three lines, and the three lines always have 5, 7, and 5 syllables each, like this:

| Leav | ing | a | vill| age | = 5 syllables
| for | life | in | a | ci | ty | is | = 7 syllables
| a | hard | change | to | make.| = 5 syllables

Now write your own haiku, one for each of the other three stories. Think about what each story is really about. What are the important ideas for you? Remember to keep to three lines of 5, 7, 5 syllables each.

ABOUT THE AUTHORS

HUSEYIN RAHMI GURPINAR

Huseyin Rahmi Gurpinar (1864–1944) was born in Istanbul in Turkey. His mother died when he was only three, and he lived with his grandmother. He went to several schools, but did not finish his studies because of illness. At different times he worked for the government, and as a writer for several newspapers. In 1912 he moved to a small wooden house on Heybelida Island, which is close to Istanbul. He never married, and lived on the island with a friend and several cats. When he died, his last words were said to be, 'Feed my cats well.'

His first novels, *Elegant* (1889) and *Chastity* (1898), made him famous, and he went on to write more than 40 novels. His stories were centred on the lives of ordinary people in Istanbul, and he wrote with black humour about their relationships and arguments, their mistakes and confusions.

AYSE KILIMCI

Ayse Kilimci (1954–) was born in Izmir in Turkey. She is a graduate of Izmir High School for Girls and Ankara Academy of Social Services. Her stories have appeared in print since 1972, and she continued her writing while also working as a social services expert at the Mersin Child Protection House. At the 1982 Peace and Friendship Award Ceremony her story *Everything Starts with Love* received a special mention. She has written many short stories, including *Children Deprived of Love* (1987) and *Rose Night Watchman* (1989). She also writes books for children. In 1995 she received the Yunus Nadi Short Story Award for her story *Epic of Fashionable Love*.

SAIT FAIK ABASIYANIK

Sait Faik (1906–1954) was born in Adapazari in Turkey. After studying at universities in Switzerland and France, he tried different jobs – businessman, teacher, journalist – but his real love was writing, and his first book of short stories, *The Samovar*, came out in 1936. He never married, and lived with his mother in the family home on Burgaz Island, near Istanbul.

Sait Faik, one of the greatest Turkish writers of short stories, wrote more than 190 stories. His stories give colourful pictures of the lives of Burgaz islanders, fishermen, priests, children, office workers, criminals . . . He was interested in everybody – good, bad, poor, unhappy, unimportant. 'I love people more than flags,' he wrote. 'Everything starts with loving a person.'

He was an honorary member of the International Mark Twain Society in the USA, and every year the Sait Faik Short Story Award is given to the best collection of short stories.

YALVAC URAL

Yalvac Ural (1945–) was born in Konya in Turkey. He works as a journalist, as an editor with many children's magazines, and is a well-known contributor to children's programmes on Turkish television. He is famous for his books for children, and has won many prizes in Turkey and abroad. He is also a musician, and a poet, writing poetry mostly for children but also for adults. In 2001 he represented Turkey at the International Children's Poetry Festival.

One of his children's books, *La Fontaine at the Forest Law Court* (1984), has been published many times, and is performed in almost every school theatre in Turkey. In 1986 he received the International Order of the Smile from children in Poland, an award for his ability to make the children of the world smile.

OXFORD BOOKWORMS LIBRARY

Classics • Crime & Mystery • Factfiles • Fantasy & Horror
Human Interest • Playscripts • Thriller & Adventure
True Stories • World Stories

The OXFORD BOOKWORMS LIBRARY provides enjoyable reading in English, with a wide range of classic and modern fiction, non-fiction, and plays. It includes original and adapted texts in seven carefully graded language stages, which take learners from beginner to advanced level. An overview is given on the next pages.

All Stage 1 titles are available as audio recordings, as well as over eighty other titles from Starter to Stage 6. All Starters and many titles at Stages 1 to 4 are specially recommended for younger learners. Every Bookworm is illustrated, and Starters and Factfiles have full-colour illustrations.

The OXFORD BOOKWORMS LIBRARY also offers extensive support. Each book contains an introduction to the story, notes about the author, a glossary, and activities. Additional resources include tests and worksheets, and answers for these and for the activities in the books. There is advice on running a class library, using audio recordings, and the many ways of using Oxford Bookworms in reading programmes. Resource materials are available on the website <www.oup.com/bookworms>.

The *Oxford Bookworms Collection* is a series for advanced learners. It consists of volumes of short stories by well-known authors, both classic and modern. Texts are not abridged or adapted in any way, but carefully selected to be accessible to the advanced student.

You can find details and a full list of titles in the *Oxford Bookworms Library Catalogue* and *Oxford English Language Teaching Catalogues*, and on the website <www.oup.com/bookworms>.

THE OXFORD BOOKWORMS LIBRARY
GRADING AND SAMPLE EXTRACTS

STARTER • 250 HEADWORDS

present simple – present continuous – imperative –
can/cannot, must – *going to* (future) – simple gerunds …

Her phone is ringing – but where is it?

Sally gets out of bed and looks in her bag. No phone. She looks under the bed. No phone. Then she looks behind the door. There is her phone. Sally picks up her phone and answers it. *Sally's Phone*

STAGE 1 • 400 HEADWORDS

… past simple – coordination with *and*, *but*, *or* –
subordination with *before*, *after*, *when*, *because*, *so* …

I knew him in Persia. He was a famous builder and I worked with him there. For a time I was his friend, but not for long. When he came to Paris, I came after him – I wanted to watch him. He was a very clever, very dangerous man. *The Phantom of the Opera*

STAGE 2 • 700 HEADWORDS

… present perfect – *will* (future) – *(don't) have to, must not, could* –
comparison of adjectives – simple *if* clauses – past continuous –
tag questions – *ask/tell* + infinitive …

While I was writing these words in my diary, I decided what to do. I must try to escape. I shall try to get down the wall outside. The window is high above the ground, but I have to try. I shall take some of the gold with me – if I escape, perhaps it will be helpful later. *Dracula*

STAGE 3 • 1000 HEADWORDS

... should, may – present perfect continuous – *used to* – past perfect
– causative – relative clauses – indirect statements ...

Of course, it was most important that no one should see Colin, Mary, or Dickon entering the secret garden. So Colin gave orders to the gardeners that they must all keep away from that part of the garden in future. ***The Secret Garden***

STAGE 4 • 1400 HEADWORDS

... past perfect continuous – passive (simple forms) –
would conditional clauses – indirect questions –
relatives with *where/when* – gerunds after prepositions/phrases ...

I was glad. Now Hyde could not show his face to the world again. If he did, every honest man in London would be proud to report him to the police. ***Dr Jekyll and Mr Hyde***

STAGE 5 • 1800 HEADWORDS

... future continuous – future perfect –
passive (modals, continuous forms) –
would have conditional clauses – modals + perfect infinitive ...

If he had spoken Estella's name, I would have hit him. I was so angry with him, and so depressed about my future, that I could not eat the breakfast. Instead I went straight to the old house. ***Great Expectations***

STAGE 6 • 2500 HEADWORDS

... passive (infinitives, gerunds) – advanced modal meanings –
clauses of concession, condition

When I stepped up to the piano, I was confident. It was as if I knew that the prodigy side of me really did exist. And when I started to play, I was so caught up in how lovely I looked that I didn't worry how I would sound. ***The Joy Luck Club***

OXFORD BOOKWORMS LIBRARY